SCHIRMER'S LIBRARY
OF MUSICAL CLASSICS

F. MAZAS

Op. 36

Seventy-Five
Melodious and Progressive
Studies

For the Violin

IN THREE BOOKS

T0057867

G. SCHIRMER, Inc.

DISTRIBUTED BY

HAL•LEONARD®
CORPORATION
7777 W. BLUEMOUND RD. P.O. BOX 13819 MILWAUKEE, WI 53213

Brilliant Studies.

Mélodie.

Adagio non troppo.

F. MAZAS. Op. 36 Book II.

The Legato.

Bowing-exercise.

The Staccato.

Melody on the G-string.

Andante sostenuto.

35.

The Martellato.
Bowing-exercise.

Firm stroke from middle to point.
Allegro moderato assai.

36.

The Arpeggio.
Bowing-exercise.

The Portamento.

Andante sostenuto.

espressivo

Bowing-exercise on two strings, for flexibility of the wrist.

Embellishments of the Melody.

Andante cantabile.

40.

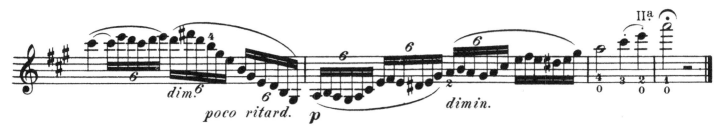

The Accented Appoggiatura.

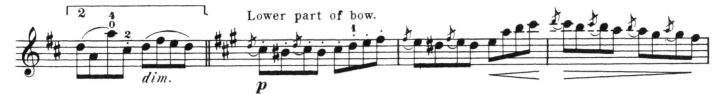

Bowing-exercise.

At the point, with short bow.

Allegro.

42.

p leggiero

Bowing-exercise.

Musette.
Andantino.

Various Bowings.

Springing Bow.

Lifting the Bow.

Staccato.

Grazioso.

Allegretto quasi Andante.

48.

Dal segno al Fine

Bowing-exercise.

Bowing-exercise.

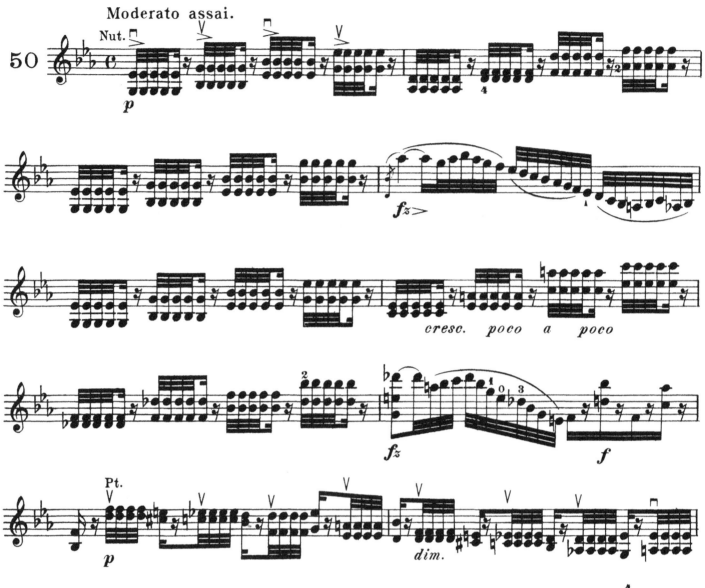

Lifting the Bow.

At the point, with very short strokes.
Allegro.

Bowing-exercise.

Well marked at the point of the bow.
Allegro non troppo.

Bowing-exercise.

53. Moderato assai.

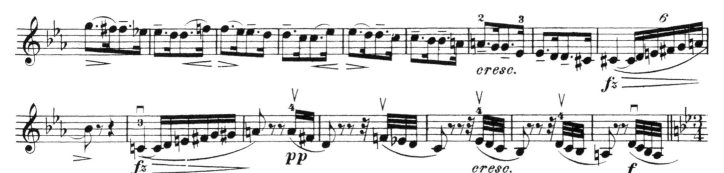

Finger-exercise.

54.

Allegro vivace.

D.C.

Trill-exercise.

Allegro moderato.

55.

Exercise on the Mordent.

Pizzicato with the left hand (indicated by +) and Harmonics.

Dal segno, senza ripresa, poi

Coda.